Anonymous

Exercises in Commemoration of the Founding of Knox

College

Held in Galesburg, Illinois, Thursday, February the Fifteenth, MDCCCXCIV

Anonymous

Exercises in Commemoration of the Founding of Knox College
Held in Galesburg, Illinois, Thursday, February the Fifteenth, MDCCCXCIV

ISBN/EAN: 9783337062491

Printed in Europe, USA, Canada, Australia, Japan

Cover: Foto ©Paul-Georg Meister /pixelio.de

More available books at **www.hansebooks.com**

EXERCISES

IN COMMEMORATION OF

THE FOUNDING

OF

KNOX COLLEGE

HELD IN

GALESBURG, ILLINOIS

THURSDAY, FEBRUARY THE FIFTEENTH

MDCCCXCIV.

GALESBURG, ILL.,:
THE MAIL PUBLISHING CO,
1894.

"WHO THAT LOVES THE SOUL OF MEN CAN LOOK ON THIS FIELD AND NOT FEEL HIS HEART AFFECTED, AND NOT TAX HIS ENERGIES TO THE UTMOST, AS WELL AS OFFER HIS MOST FERVENT PRAYERS TO THE LORD OF THE HARVEST, THAT HE WOULD FURNISH THE LABORERS? WHO THAT LOVES THE INSTITUTIONS OF HIS COUNTRY, CAN LOOK UPON IT WITHOUT ALARM, WHEN HE REFLECTS THAT IN A FEW, A VERY FEW YEARS, THEY WILL BE IN THE HANDS OF A POPULATION REARED IN THIS FIELD ; AND REARED, UNLESS A MIGHTY EFFORT BE MADE BY EVANGELICAL CHRISTIANS, UNDER THE FORMING HAND OF THOSE WHO ARE NO LESS THE ENEMIES OF CIVIL LIBERTY, THAN OF A PURE GOSPEL?"   GEORGE W. GALE.

(EXTRACT FROM "CIRCULAR AND PLAN" 1836.)

TO THE
MEMORY
OF
THE FOUNDERS.

PREFATORY NOTE.

The public exercises in celebration of the fifty-seventh anniversary of the Founding of Knox College took place on Thursday, February 15th, 1894. The morning exercises were held in the Old First Church. The addresses made on that occasion, memorable because of the addresses, will be found within. In the afternoon a complimentary entertainment was given in the Presbyterian Church by the Conservatory of Music and the Department of Elocution, under the direction of Prof. W. F. Bentley, the Director of the Conservatory, and Miss Grace Chamberlain. In the evening an address was delivered in the Presbyterian Church by the Hon. George R. Peck, of Chicago. This eloquent and inspiring address is published in full in this brochure. After the address a reception was given in the parlors of the church by the Trustees and Faculty of the College.

The addresses are published by order of the Executive Committee of the Board of Trustees.

PROGRAM.

— OF —

KNOX COLLEGE FOUNDERS' DAY.

MORNING EXERCISES.

OLD FIRST CHURCH

10 O'CLOCK A. M.

Mr. John H. Finley, Presiding.

Music,	Knox College Cadet Band
Invocation,	Dr. A. F. Sherrill
Greeting from the City,	Mayor F. F. Cooke
The Founders,	Hon. W. Selden Gale
Early Days,	Prof. George Churchill
Sons and Daughters of Knox,	Dr. C. W. Leffingwell
(Rector St. Mary's School.)	
Sisters of Knox,	Dr. John E. Bradley
(President Illinois College.)	
Song, "Ave Maria"—Faure,	Mrs. F. J. Bentley
The Mission of the Christian College,	Rev. Wm. S. Marquis
(Pastor Presbyterian Church, Rock Island.)	
The College and the Church,	Rev. C. W. Hiatt
(Pastor First Congregational Church, Peoria.)	
The College and the University,	Dr. Albion W. Small
(University of Chicago.)	
Song—"To Sing the Praise of Dear old Knox"	Students
The Value of a College Education,	Hon. L. S. Coffin
The Future of Our College,	Prof. Albert Hurd
Founders' Day Hymn. (Composed by Prof. L. S. Pratt.)	
Benediction,	Rev. E. G. Smith
Music,	Knox College Cadet Band

AFTERNOON EXERCISES.

PRESBYTERIAN CHURCH

2 O'CLOCK P. M.

Complimentary Entertainment Given by the Knox Conservatory of Music and the Department of Elocution to the Citizens of Galesburg and the Students of Knox College.

1 Petite Suite for String Orchestra, - - *George Saint-George*
   I. Preludio.   II. Allemanda.   III. Sarabanda.   IV. Minuetto 1st;
   Minuetto 2d.   V. Bourree.   VI. Giga.
         KNOX CONSERVATORY STRING ORCHESTRA.

2 SELECTION—From Tennyson's "Idylls":
         Part I—Gareth at the Court of Arthur.
         MISS GRACE CHAMBERLAIN.

3 SONG—"Were I the Streamlet," - - - *C. Francis Lloyd*
         MISS SARAH L. BARNDT.

4 STRING ORCHESTRA—(*a*) Herzwunden, } - - - *Grieg*
                    (*b*) Der Fruhling, }

5 ORGAN SOLO—Concert theme, with variations in G, - *Guilmant*
         PROF. F. W. MUELLER.

6 SONG—Doris (a Pastorale), - - - - *Ethelbert Nevin*
         (Accompaniment for Piano, Violin and "Cello,"
         MISS FLORENCE J. LEE.

7 SELECTION—Part II.—Gareth's Quests.
         MISS CHAMBERLAIN.

8 STRING ORCHESTRA—Intermezzo from Cavalleria Rusticana,
                    - - - - - - - *Mascagni*
         (Organ Accompaniment.)

PROGRAM—(CON.)

EVENING EXERCISES.

PRESBYTERIAN CHURCH

8 O'CLOCK P. M.

HON. CLARK E. CARR, Presiding.

ORGAN SOLO—"Festival March,"   -   -   ·   -   *Henry Smart*

PROF. F. W. MUELLER.

INTRODUCTORY ADDRESS,   -   -   -   -   HON. CLARK E. CARR

ADDRESS,   -   -   -   -   -   -   HON. GEORGE R. PECK

"THE KINGDOM OF LIGHT."

*"It is a fortunate thing for this institution that it is located in a region to which nature has given her kindliest smiles; a land of meadow and of garden, and of goodly people living in goodly homes. * * * I cannot help thinking that the subtle law of heredity has played a powerful part in the success which has hitherto attended the work of Knox College. * * * The iron which was in the blood of the pioneers gives tone and vigor to the students of to-day. * * * What Knox will do in the future depends upon the character of the teachers who fill the chairs, but, after all, the students themselves must set the mark of the institution."*

(Col. George R. Peck, in Founder's Day Address.)

I would give more for the ideals, the purposes of the men and women whose lives have gone into the structure of this College than for all the libraries that wealth can buy.

(Dr. Small, in Founders' Day Address.)

KNOX COLLEGE FOUNDERS' DAY.

At half past nine o'clock on the morning of Founders' Day the trustees of the college, the guests of the day, the faculty and the students formed a line at Alumni Hall and marched across the park to the Old First Church, the college cadet band leading the march with music, the classes challenging one another with the college yell and displaying flags and streamers of purple and old gold. The "Old First" was filled; the students on one side of the house, the townspeople and other friends on the other side. The stage was tastefully decorated and an oil painting of General Knox, loaned by Mrs. F. C. Rice, a great-grand daughter, hung at one side. The cadet band played an overture, after which the chairman, President Finley, spoke a few words of welcome to those who had come to celebrate the day with the faculty and students, and said: "When the Legislature at Vandalia was voting on this day, fifty-seven years ago, to charter Knox College, the colonists at "Log City" were taking the first steps toward the organization of a church, the church under whose ample roof we are met today. This is, then, the birthday, too, of this church. It is fitting, therefore, that the first voice raised this morning in thanksgiving for the past should be that of the pastor of this old church, which has been so closely associated with the college in the memory of her students. Dr. A. F. Sherrill will lead us in prayer to the God who led our fathers to these prairies."

PRAYER BY REV. A. F. SHERRILL, D. D.

O Lord our God, our fathers trusted in Thee and were not ashamed. They came here and builded well. They placed the college and church side by side—they fostered good industries. They laid broad and deep foundations for good society, for true and enduring welfare. We thank thee for them and their labors into which we enter; may we follow their good example. May thy blessing be upon us as we come together on this Founders' Day, and into this house hallowed by scenes and memories of the past. Make all hearts glad while the sky and natural world around us are telling of thy glory. May the special object which has called us together be accomplished. May we see and realize the critical time which has come to our beloved college; may we call it our opportunity, and may many hearts be quickened to new interest and to generous giving, so that this noble institution of Christian learning shall not be divided in its works but gain large means of power and usefulness. May old friends remain and be strong; may new ones be added, and from this hour may there date new interest, enthusiasm, devotion, which shall only increase with the growing years. And may all the learning, all the money, all the lives, be consecrated to the good of one another and to the glory of thy great name. Amen.

The Chairman: This day is the birthday not only of the college and the church but also of the city of Galesburg. To plant here on the prairies a Christian institution of learning was the object foremost in the minds and the plans of the colonists. Around this college the town was planted and so the "College City" may well celebrate with us this day. I regret, and I bring the regrets of the present Mayor of our beautiful city, that he cannot himself give the greeting of the citizens of Galesburg, but the presence of so many of you here this morning with our students and your interest in the growth of the college, expressed in many and helpful ways, give evidence of the cordiality of the greeting you have in your hearts for the institution which is walled in by your houses and shops—We are gathered to-day to pay tribute to the memory of those who gave us Knox College—the Pilgrim Fathers of our little community, and I know of no one who could more fittingly speak the first words than the son of its founder, the "first citizen" of Galesburg to-day—the Hon. W. Selden Gale, whom I now have the pleasure and honor of introducing to you. He will speak concerning

"THE FOUNDERS OF KNOX."

Mr. Chairman, Ladies and Gentlemen:

The germ from which Knox College grew may be found in the village of Western, Oneida county, N. Y., in the year 1825. George W. Gale was born in 1789. He was the son of one of those men who in colonial times crossed the Connecticut border to occupy the land between

New England and the Dutch settlements on the Hudson. At the time of his birth that emigration had passed up the great river of New England to New Connecticut, as they called it, and founded the State of Vermont. Connecticut men had begun to settle the country above the Dutch settlements on the Mohawk. Hugh White and his sons had just begun to clear the forests for Whitesboro', the oldest village in the western half of New York, the cradle of Knox College. Mr. Gale, an orphan at an early age, affectionately cared for by older sisters, the wives of thrifty farmers, trained to habits of industry and given such advantages of education as were available, graduated from the college and the theological seminary which New England men had founded in Schenectady and Princeton. After being licensed to preach, his first mission was to the new settlements near Lake Ontario; his first settlement, at what was then the thriving town and is now the pretty village of Adams; his parishioners enterprising villagers and energetic farmers. At thirty-five years of age, to his great disappointment and the regret of those he served, who loved him, his health gave way. Compelled to abandon his profession—he feared forever—he found a retreat in a small village on an estate belonging to a lawyer who had left it for a time; a beautiful situation, a few acres of land, and, in the old style of the professional man's establishment, an office on the street at the foot of the lawn.

With habits formed in an education by those to whom idleness was reckoned a crime, he could not be without occupation, and soon he had half a dozen students for the ministry about him. They read his books, they came to his table, they worked his land. Two years he spent in Western. It was at that time that the great religious revival swept like a prairie fire over central and western New York. It brought to the surface the so well known Charles G. Finney, who dropped the law for the gospel while chorister in Mr. Gale's church at Adams, and got his first theological reading in Mr. Gale's library.

Mr. Gale left Western with some ideas. Sharing, though with his characteristic moderation, in the religious enthusiasm of the day, he deeply felt the want of educated ministers to provide for the new congregations in the growing country. The young men on the farms and in the shops who, by natural talents, were well adapted to the ministry—for these he wished to provide better educational facilities. He attributed his loss of health to the change of habits, going from active life on the farm to the sedentary life of a student—a danger which he thought should be carefully guarded against. Athletic games and exercises might have seemed a wasteful misuse of time and strength to one trained to think all time must be profitably or usefully spent. He thought a college might be established where the students could be provided with labor for a portion of each day, securing the necessary healthful exercise and help to pay their way.

There were in that day few men of wealth, as wealth is estimated now, but there were men well-to-do, enterprising and religious. Able to gain the confidence of such men, by personal solicitations Mr. Gale collected enough money to buy 100 acres of land, to erect buildings with suitable rooms for college exercises, dormitories—then a necessary part of college outfit—for 100 students; various other buildings; some books and apparatus, and some endowment for professors. The students in classes, with monitors chosen by themselves, were employed three hours each day in farming or gardening, except some who had trades, for whom shops were provided. Three hours' work paid for board and room-rent. The government was a regular democracy—the monitors in meeting managed affairs, with little oversight by the faculty. Young men coming from farms and shops and some from wealthy parents who liked the system, brought together under the religious excitement that prevailed and the temperance and abolition excitement that followed, were generally more mature than usual in college, and I will venture to say that no greater amount of either enthusiasm or brains was ever brought together in any college with equal numbers. As a training school for debaters it was unequaled. Its most brilliant specimen was Theodore D. Weld.

Mr. Gale never intended to spend his life teaching. He got the institution to running so it paid its expenses, and having secured good hands, as he thought, to leave it in, he retired after six years' connection. At that time the westward movement of population continued with accelerated force. The favorite field with New Yorkers was Michigan. Mr. Gale had developed more ideas. In the west where land had but a nominal cost, the outfit for a manual labor college would be greatly reduced. The west was the coming field; it would be well to prepare for the work on the ground where the work was to be done. He had seen all his life land advancing in value with increase of population. He saw in that the means of college endowment. He thought the advance might be greatly hastened if settlers would move in a body, taking with them what made the difference between an old settlement and a new. If land, he said, is worth $1.25 per acre where settlements are sparse, it will be worth at least $5.00 per acre with schools, churches and good so-

REV. HIRAM H. KELLOGG, D. D.

ciety. His plan was to secure the settlers, purchase a township of government land at $1.25, parcel it out to the settlers at $5.00 and with the profits establish the schools. Such attractions would draw together those who could appreciate them. Before he left the Oneida Institute, I have seen in his study plans of a township and village in Michigan. After leaving the Institute much of his time was devoted to correspondence, visiting friends who would sympathize with him, or might take part in such work. He knew what making a farm in heavily timbered lands involved, and reflection and examination satisfied him that in the prairies of northern Illinois there was a fairer field than even the beautiful oak openings of Michigan. He found ready co-operation in his associates in the Presbytery. The most active and efficient assistance came from Rev. Hiram H. Kellogg, who had established a ladies' seminary, in some respects a counterpart of the Oneida Institute, and who afterward became the first president of Knox College. At the close of 1834 the plan had been developed and a subscription begun. Among the first to join was one who became the backbone of the enterprise—Silvanus Ferris. A personal friend and by marriage a relation of Mr. Gale, forty years before, with his axe and little wealth besides, with a lovely young wife (I knew her when she was no longer young—what she was in her girlhood those still older than she have told me), he passed White's settlement, where Whitesboro' was to be, and cut out of the dense forest his farm. There he was a pioneer in that cheese industry that has spread from the town of Norway over the counties around. With marvelous industry he had acquired a handsome property, when, at sixty-four, with the buoyancy of youth, he joined the expedition, and for twenty-five years was one of the chief builders of the college. May 6th, 1835, at the Presbyterian church in Rome, the subscribers to Mr. Gale's plan met and organized, appointed a managing committee, and Mr. Gale general agent. Nehemiah West, Thomas Gilbert and Timothy B. Jarvis were appointed a committee, instructed to explore Indiana and Illinois between the 40th and 42nd degrees of latitude and to find a suitable location where an entire township of government land might be procured. The committee reported that they had not been able to find a suitable location, and, as land was being rapidly taken up advised that a committee be sent out with funds to buy a half township, as soon as one could be found. Mr. Gilbert bought for himself land two miles south of Knoxville and reported that half a township might be had there. The report was discouraging; the amount of land in half a township seemed too small to effect what was desired, but at a meeting held August 19, 1835, Mr. Gale, Mr. Ferris, Mr. West and Mr. Simmons were directed to proceed, find and purchase half a township, and were provided with funds for the purpose. The committee, except Mr. Gale, who was left sick at Detroit, went to Knoxville as advised by Mr. Gilbert. They stopped with Dr. Hansford, the veteran pioneer, the first physician settled in Knox county, and at that time the proprietor of half the town plat of Knoxville. Learning their errand, he proposed to show them all the land they wanted, and lying between Knoxville and Henderson Grove they found as fair a prairie as the sun shone on. Their satisfaction was mingled with regret when they found they might have had the full complement of land if they had come prepared. On the 7th of January, 1836, the subscribers' meeting at Whitesboro received the committee's report. They approved a plan laying out the purchase—the town plat in the center and lands adjoining reserved for the college. The remaining lands were appraised at from $3 to $8, according to location, averaging $5. Each made his selection, bidding for choice when there was competition. The proceeds of sales, it was agreed, should first cover the expense of purchasing; the remainder, with all lands unsold, to be conveyed to the college when incorporated, meantime remaining with the committee in trust.

In the spring of 1836 the colonists began to arrive at the purchase. With them came friends, who, pleased with the scheme, joined in. Others came in from New York, and a company from Vermont, headed by Matthew Chambers and Erastus Swift, looking for homes in the west, were attracted to the colony and became part of it. The first settlers found shelter at Henderson Grove; some in the cabins of the settlers, who within the seven years before had lined the Grove with a tier of farms; some erected cabins on colony land at the Grove.

On the 15th day of February, 1837, the charter of Knox College was granted.

Before the close of 1836 about forty families connected with the colony had arrived; the Presbyterian church was organized in a small building erected for the purpose. Prof. Losey opened a school, the real beginning of Knox College; and here let me mention the good fortune of Knox College and Galesburg, that among the men brought to Oneida Institute by Mr. Gale and who followed him to Galesburg, were two men, accomplished scholars and teachers of great ability, who gave the college its original form and prestige and impressed upon it the characteristics that have marked it in all its history—Nehemiah H. Losey and Inness Grant; one a graduate of Middlebury, the other of Aberdeen. Mr. Losey came in 1836 as teacher, surveyor, accountant; his services were indispensable. Prof. Grant came when the college needed a professor of languages. In 1836 the building of Galesburg on the prairie began. The school was opened never to be closed. In 1846, in this house, then unfinished, was graduated the first senior class of Knox College.

I will not go further. I have followed the founders of the college. It is to their credit that they laid so firm a foundation on which so fair a fabric has been raised. At the very outset the character of the founders drew to them co-workers of like principles and tastes. The institutions they founded which they and their associates have built, have continued to draw those who can appreciate such institutions. That influence will continue; the characteristics will be permanent; Knox College will be surrounded by a cultured people.

The Chairman: We have among our faculty several immortals; men whose memories will never die at Knox. One of these is Professor George Churchill, Emperor of all the "Preps," and King of all our hearts. Though he seems as young as any of us, he has a memory and experience which cover the whole history of Galesburg and of Knox College. He will tell us of the "good old days."

"EARLY DAYS."

Ladies and Gentlemen, Citizens and Students:

With a plan so wisely and carefully prepared, in the hands of men chosen for their peculiar adaptation to their several duties, and all inspired with the grand purpose of planting Christian educational institutions to aid in shaping the character of the coming empire of the "far west," success seemed inevitable, and success did come, but through continuous years of hard labor by the founders, teachers and the entire band of colonists who had been drawn hither by their faith in the plan, their desire to aid in its prosecution and their hope of participation in the benefits arising from its accomplishment. Log City was the temporary home of the colonists and its name indicates the primitive character of their dwellings. It was built in the grove three miles northwest from the college site. As soon as these shelters were built a meeting house of "shakes" was erected, in which to have a school on work

days and a place for worship on Sundays. In this meeting house, during
the first winter, was held a series of meetings that resulted in the conver-
sion of most of the young folks in the colony. At the close of these
meetings, on February 15, 1837, just fifty-seven years ago to-day, the colonists held a meeting to organize a church, and on the same day the
state legislature in Vandalia, then the capital of the state, granted a
charter to Knox College. So the college and the church were born on
the same day—were twins, and in their early history they were one and
inseparable, devoted to a common cause, laboring for each other, sharing the common burdens and rejoicing together over the common suc-
cesses. In spite of the hard times caused by the panic of 1837, the colonists one after another moved out upon the prairie and built houses.
The prairie upon which the city stands was a typical prairie, a thing of
beauty which none but those who have actually seen a virgin prairie in
all its changing dress of green, its moods of sunshine and shades as the
clouds pass over its surface, can fully appreciate. When the village had
been laid out and the site of the college determined, a few of the founders met upon the site and with uncovered heads knelt down, and the
oldest one of the group, with his long, white hair streaming in the wind,
gave thanks to God, and with impassioned earnestness, dedicated the
beautiful prairie, the village, and the college the center of all, to the
Lord.

I fully believe that prayer was heard and the dedication accepted by
the Lord, for the enterprise grew apace, the village grew, new colonists
came and in November, 1838, the college was at home for the first time
in its first building, now familiarly called "The Old Academy", which
stood just where the First National Bank now stands, and is now the
residence of Mr. A. Nelson, the second house north of the bank. This
building was shared by college and church alike, and was the place
where the colonists were wont to assemble to hear passing lectur-
ers, and to discuss all the great reforms of the day, for they were
leaders in the anti-slavery movement, in the temperance cause, in the
work of missions at home and abroad, and all other causes in keeping
with their great plan of helping to shape for good the character of the
coming western empire. From the first occupancy of their building, revival followed revival, in which church and college alike were equal act-
ors and equal recipients of the attendant blessings, until the building
seemed the very gate of heaven to the many who, within its walls, had
first felt the grace of God in their hearts.

PROFESSOR NEHEMIAH H. LOSEY.

The atmosphere was a safe one for young people to live in and for all, both young and old, to breathe, to enjoy, and to grow better in. Strangers in the place at once felt the presence of something that inspired all that was good in them and repressed all that was evil. A story is told of a man, who, passing through the village in the stage and being much pleased with everything around him, asked the driver what kind of a place this was, and the man answered that it was such a place that he did not dare to swear at his horses anywhere in sight of it.

As I call up my boyhood memories of the first few years of the school, one man stands in the forefront as the real presiding genius of the school and that man was Prof. N. H. Losey. He was an "all 'round man," good in everything; could teach Greek and Latin if necessary, was thoroughly at home in mathematics, quick and accurate in his calculations, remarkably clear and concise in his explanations, showing up the curiosities and mysteries of mathematics in such a way as to arouse all the enthusiasm there was in his pupils. I think it is especially due to Prof. N. H. Losey that Knox College has from the first taken high rank in its teaching of mathematics. But not in this line was Prof. Losey's great power during the first few years of the school; it was rather in physics and chemistry that he excelled. With almost no apparatus to begin with, in a short time he had constructed such laboratory appliances as to enable him to show off the wonders of those sciences in such a way as to attract large numbers of scholars from the surrounding country. He was as truly the wizard of Knox College at that time as is Edison the wizard of Menlo Park today. When he lectured on chemistry not only the students and the colonists were attentive listeners, but the people from the groves round about came for miles and gazed with wonder and admiration at his experiments with electricity, olefiant gas, laughing gas, and magic lantern shows of things comical and instructive. Then, too, he was a good organizer, a strict disciplinarian, a good manager and always a true gentleman.

I have spoken of Prof. Losey as one whose life and labors had great influence in giving a decided character for good to the school. In this line the name of Prof. Inness Grant should always be associated with that of Prof. Losey; not that the two men were alike, for they were totally unlike, and yet each had the power to inspire and lead young men into their respective fields of study. Prof. Grant was a Scotchman, possessing to the full all the sterling virtues of his nature, quaint in his language, always saying just what he meant and saying it so that the hearer had no trouble in understanding the pith of the matter; a man with profound convictions on the great questions of the day and fearless in the expression of these opinions. He despised men of mere pretense but admired those who lived and acted under a true devotion to duty. His ringing speeches to the students to work because it was their duty to themselves, to their parents, to their friends and to God, inspired hundreds of them and made them nobler and better men.

I never pass by the "Old Academy" without a flood of memories of the early days coming over me, and I often wonder if the members of the family now occupying it as a residence do not sometimes, in the stillness of the night, when the ghosts of the departed are flitting through the rooms, hear the walls echoing the orthodox sermons, the eloquent anti-slavery speeches, the sound advice given to students, the eloquent orations of the upper classmen and the still more eloquent declamations of the lower classmen, to say nothing of the incipient efforts of "prep. dom," with which the walls and ceiling of the house must be thoroughly charged.

Early in the "forties" the Old Academy became too small to accommodate the audiences that gathered to hear the college exhibitions, lectures or other entertainments, as well as the congregations on the Sabbath. Hence, college, church and citizens determined to provide a building that should be ample for all such gatherings, and especially for the college commencements that would soon put in an appearance. The outcome of this determination was this church building in which we are to-day assembled—at that time the largest audience room in the state outside of Chicago. The first audience ever assembled in the building was at the first commencement of Knox College, in June, 1846, when nine young men were graduated: Bush, Davis, Hitchcock, Holyoke, Leonard, Martin, Olney, Richardson and Smith were the immortal *nine*; men good and true, who have done grand work in three continents. Five of them have gone to their reward and four remain, whose faces are often seen at the annual commencement exercises of the college.

The day was a great one for Galesburg. All rejoiced; founders, faculty, students and citizens, for they were sending out their first corps of trained men to fight life's battles, and from that day until now Knox has not failed to add its annual companies of young men, armed and equipped to do good work in the world.

For many years this old building was the place where all assemblies of the people, religious, educational or political were held. Here sang the Hutchinsons and the Alleghanians; here lectured the most distinguished platform orators of America invited to Galesburg by the students, and here during the civil war Chaplain McCabe and others equally eloquent made speeches that still ring in the ears of those who heard them.

This evening you will be called into another church, one of the most beautiful in this part of Illinois, which will show what an influence Knox College has had in educating the community architecturally.

I have been more or less intimately connected with the College from its very beginning. I as a lad of ten years was a pupil in the first year of the school and am now in my thirty-ninth year of consecutive service as an instructor. My life has been spent in the school and I am proud of it. And now as I am going toward the sunset of life, I am constrained to look backward and review the scenes in which I have been a participant. I go back to the wild prairie, beautiful in its summer suns; I see the billows of flame roll over its surface as the fire licks up the dry grass; I see the works of man covering the surface of the country; the growing crops and trees; the houses dropping down and taking on the cozy look of the New England homes; the little community transforming itself into a village and then into a small city, connected with other cities by nerves of wire and bands of steel, and all these signs of thrift and comfort gathered around the college and largely its product; then, too, I see a long procession of young people coming up from all parts of the land, that they may drink deeply of the waters of the Pierian spring and go forth to all quarters of the earth to give to others what they have received here. The vision is an inspiring one and a satisfactory one. I wish you could all see what I now see as I close my eyes and dream of the past of Knox College. May its future be as bright as the wishes of its founders and builders ever desired it to be.

The Chairman: Knox has sons and daughters now, almost a thousand, young and old, and she is fond and proud of them. For this great family of children, children some of them with gray heads, one of them, beloved of the mother and kept near her, will speak to-day, the Rev. C. W. Leffingwell, D. D., Rector of St. Mary's School, Knoxville, Ill., and editor of *The Living Church*.

"THE SONS AND DAUGHTERS OF KNOX."

Mr. Chairman, Ladies and Gentlemen:

Like every good mother, our *Alma Mater* when she celebrates her birthday, remembers her children, and it is because they are loyal and true that she is able to keep this day with rejoicing.   Old Mother Knox has many sons and daughters, aye, and grandchildren too, who are wishing her many happy returns of the day.

We are not ashamed of the Knox family wherever found, and they are found in almost every part of the civilized world—and in Florida. These true, earnest, helpful men and women are at work, and have been for half a century, in places of trust, in Christian schools and homes, in all the enterprises with which a prosperous nation abounds.   They have filled places of honor and of danger, not hesitating to respond to the call of country in the hour of peril.   Among the graves that are gratefully visited on Decoration Day there are none more worthy of honor than those where sleep the soldier boys of Knox.

The roll call of the Alumni–æ (if I may coin a word to include the graduates of both sides of the park), would suggest a record of noble service and good report, of which any college might be proud.   It is not, however, upon the record of a few exceptionally brilliant careers that we congratulate Knox College to-day, but upon the honorable and useful lives which she has helped so many hundreds to live, yea, upon the thousands who have gone forth bearing good seed and using the intellectual and moral powers which were trained here for the benefit of mankind.

So it seems right and good that *Alma Mater*, when she looks back over her many years of honorable service, should remember the sons and daughters whom God hath given her as the crown and glory of her work, and they upon their part, should remember what they owe to their scholastic mother, "Like mother, like child."   Let the mother have credit and praise.   She desires to honor her children to-day by calling out, as I have feebly voiced it, some witness to their worth and work. This worth and work are largely the result of her training and influence, the product of what scientists call "environment."   There may be some here who can bear witness as to what this has been from the beginning, who can tell us under what auspices of faith, hope and love the college was founded and what it owes to the noble ideals of its founder, whose good stewardship we commemorate today.   My own observation extends over one generation.   It is nearly thirty years since I entered the senior class of the college.   There was then as there is now, a faculty of devoted and learned men and women deeply interested in the progress and welfare of the students.   We knew each other in those days.   I hope that Knox will never be so large and lofty that she cannot reach down and

take her children by the hand.   The inspiration that comes to youth by
association with great men is of more value than any study of books.

Thirty-three years ago! and shall I tell you what sort of men I
found in the college at that time?   They were, for the most part, earnest, hard-working students, high-minded and serious, as facing the great
issues of life.   Those were the days of the war, when old men seldom
smiled, and young men checked their laughter.   But there were many
hours of pleasant companionship and quiet enjoyment in the old barracks,
which were known as "The Bricks," and sometimes the banquet table was
spread, with peanuts in the shell and cider out of a tin cup.   That was all
the carousing I ever heard of in those days.   There was very little need
of discipline.   Sometimes a boy was sent up to the president for play-
ing some foolish prank, but there were no "bummers," no loafers in college or academy; no "lewd fellows of the baser sort" to annoy and dis-
grace the mother who was giving them shelter and training.   When I
read of the outrages committed in some institutions, it seems to me it
would be well to add to the litany for use in colleges, "From all roughs
and toughs, good Lord deliver us!"

We sons and daughters of Knox College, upon this Founders' Day
and on many other days, should not only recall the old scenes of our
life and work here; we should also try to realize what fruit that life and
work have borne in our subsequent career.   The young man who goes
"so smug upon the mart" with his diploma in hand, with his college bills
paid, may think that he owes no man anything; indeed, may fancy that
he has conferred a favor upon the college by giving it his "patronage."
The time will come, however, when he will realize to some extent what
the college has done for him; that without its training and influence he
would have been handicapped all through the race of life; that he would
have lived and moved, and had his intellectual being on a lower plane;
that he would have failed of the accomplishment of things which are his
chief honor and pride; that he would have been poor in that which he
counts his most enjoyable and durable earthly riches—the treasures of a
cultivated mind.   All these advantages have come to him, and could
have come to him only through the organic life and specialized functions
of the institution of which, for a time, he was a member.   It is a gospel
truth: "No   man   liveth   to   himself."   In   another   phase: "No
man   groweth   by   himself."   Institutions,   schools,   colleges,   churches, nations, the individual inherits.   He does not make them or re-
turn value received when he pays his bills; he only shares in some in-

cidental expenses. The foundation on which he builds was laid long ago; and some of the far-sighted founders we commemorate today; the walls and roof and furnishings and endowments, have been the result of generations of wise benefactors. Therefore, with grateful recognition of benefits received, should every son and daughter of Knox recall the founders and benefactors of an institution which has done so much for them and for the world.

As one of the sons I am glad to bring my tribute of appreciation and gratitude, and I believe that I voice the feelings and convictions of thousands in all that I have said. The Alumni of Knox have done something from time to time to express their appreciation in more substantial form than words. They will do more that way, I trust. But in one direction they have "exceeded the sum of all accounts;" they have furnished the college from their ranks a president who has the distinguished honor of being the youngest man who has ever been placed at the head of an American college of high rank. Let them now use their influence to sustain him in carrying forward the work in which some of the foremost educators in the country have preceded him, among whom, *facile princeps*, is Newton Bateman, Doctor of Laws, for more than a generation the most conspicuous among the leaders of education in Illinois, and for nearly twenty years the loved and honored president of Knox College. The sons and daughters of Knox thank God for the benediction of his presence, and for the splendid example of a long life devoted to the true, the beautiful, and the good. *Serus in cœlum redeat.*

When I note that, to-day, in active service, there are two instructors in the college, to whose lectures of more than thirty years ago I owe so much, to whom then I looked up as to men of advanced years and learning, I begin to feel young again. There is Professor Hurd, my ideal of a live teacher; I can never think of him as growing old; and Professor Comstock, whose ability to calculate an eclipse filled me with admiring wonder when I was an undergraduate, still going on as serenely as the moon; and Professor Churchill, the sturdy veteran who has stood by the Academy all these years,—but I must not speak of the fathers. The sons and daughters of Knox! Speaking for them of *Alma Mater*, I am sure that they all join me in saying that we honor her past, we admire her present, we glory in her future. Her real endowment is not in bonds and real estate, but in the consecration of noble lives to her service. In promoting her interest we honor ourselves, we honor our country, we strengthen the foundations of an institution which has long been a power for good,

PROFESSOR INNESS GRANT.

The Chairman: And Knox has sisters, too, many and · good sisters. There is one who is especially dear to her because she has given to us him who is universally beloved by the students of Knox College and our townspeople, and respected all up and down this state, Dr. Newton Bateman. We are honored today by the presence of the husband of that sister, President Bradley, of Illinois College. I have great pleasure in introducing him to you.

"SISTERS OF KNOX."

Mr. Chairman, Ladies and Gentlemen:

·We always consider it to a man's credit if he thinks a good deal of his brothers and sisters. If he is so self-centered as to take no interest in those who stand in close relationship to him we wonder if he realizes how much he is losing. Colleges are like men and I have been glad to see of late some quickening of these family ties among the colleges of this state. We had a better family reunion, it is said, at Springfield in December than had ever been held before. And soon after that Knox College showed her sisterly affection for Illinois College by sending one of her most honored and beloved instructors, Professor Hurd, to assist us in carrying on our Bible Institute.

And so I am glad to bring you the greeting of Illinois College on this happy occasion. Few institutions have better grounds for sisterly affection than Knox College and her staid elder sister Illinois. I cannot forget that after distinguished services in the cause of education in this state and throughout the country, an honored son of Illinois became president of Knox College, guiding her growth during a critical period and, at length, amid universal regret resigning the office upon which he had conferred such honor. Nor can I forget that another son of Illinois, who for more than a quarter of a century ranked perhaps, as Chicago's most eminent divine has long adorned your board of trustees, Rev. Dr. R. W. Patterson; nor that another trustee of Knox is a graduate of Illinois and a son of its illustrious president, Dr. Sturtevant.

But interesting and precious as are these ties of relationship we have far deeper and more significant reasons for mutual interest.

The establishment of American colleges by the pioneer settlers of this country is one of the most remarkable facts of American history. Harvard College was founded within six years after the planting of the Massachusetts Bay Colony. Scarcely four thousand settlers were scattered along the Massachusetts coast. No adequate provision had yet been made for their bodily comfort or their spiritual wants. But no limitations of outward circumstances could blind their eyes to the importance of intelligent and upright leadership. They feared, we are told, the influence of an ignorant clergy. They resolved that the new nation should rest upon the foundations of Christian learning. Their lofty enterprise rose above the sordid greed of gold. And so they founded a college and voted to give four hundred pounds from their meager funds for its endowment, and they wrote upon its corner stone the noble motto which still stands upon the seal of that honored institution: "*Christo et Ecclesiae.*"

Yale College was a child of a like purpose. Ten ministers met at Branford to plan for the establishment of a college for the education of Christian pastors. Each brought a few books and as he laid them on the table he said: "I give these books to found a Christian College."

And so of the fair sisterhood of colleges all over the land. They were established to promote and perpetuate a Christian education. They illustrate the foresight and consecration of their noble founders. Pre-eminently true is this of the early colleges of the west. The founders of Knox and Beloit and Iowa and Illinois looked forward to the development of the great west and calmly planned for a national destiny of which few had then conceived. There is no fairer page in American history than that which records the formation of the famous Yale band of 1829 and their consecrated enterprise in the planting of Illinois College. It was their courage and sagacity with that of men of like spirit in other places which saved Illinois and all this fair region from the curse of slavery and disseminated the spirit of the New England fathers all over this land of promise.

Knox and Illinois then are sisters not merely in that each is seeking to promote in its own sphere the cause of higher education and sound learning, but pre-eminently because of their identity in spirit and origin, because the gifts of their founders and benefactors, the life and devotion of their officers and instructors have been inwrought into their history and their present power for good. And so we do well to-day to honor the memory and the consecration of the founders of Knox. And we do well to hope that their spirit will long be shared by men of wealth and foresight all over our land.

In bringing you, then, to-day the greetings of Illinois College, I but express the sentiment and the spirit which have ruled from the first in all this fair circle of colleges. May the good Providence which guided their planting grant them a continuous and vigorous growth; may the vast population so soon to flourish here, flowing in upon these prairies in refluent waves, find that science and religion, truth and the fear of God are fostered and maintained by these pioneer institutions of Christian training.

Continuing, President Bradley alluded to the fact that there are relationships *within* colleges as well as *among* them, and as Knox had recently taken to herself a vigorous young husband, the sister colleges wished them much happiness and prosperity in the new union and hoped all Alumni and friends of Knox College would help its young president in the great and trying work of enlarging its financial resources. In this as in all worthy efforts the sister colleges bid Knox College godspeed.

Mrs. Frederick J. Bentley, of Galesburg, a great-great-grand daughter of General Henry Knox, whose name the college bears, added greatly to the enjoyment and interest of the exercises by singing "Ave Maria" (by Faure), accompanied by Prof. W. F. Bentley and Mr. Warren Willard.

The Chairman: We have neighbors, too, as well as relatives, and one of our nearest neighbors is Rock Island. It is a great pleasure to have with us to-day a good representative of that city, and of our neighbors in general, the Rev. W. S. Marquis, who will speak to

"THE MISSION OF THE CHRISTIAN COLLEGE IN AMERICA."

Ladies and Gentlemen:

When the revered Dr. Hopkins took the President's Chair at Williams in 1836, he said in his inaugural address: "I have no ambition to build up here what would be called a great institution, but I do desire and shall labor that this may be a *safe* college—that here may be health and cheerful study, and kind feelings and pure morals; and that in the memory of future students college life may be made a still more verdant spot." And no man ever redeemed a promise more nobly. Character was the thing he aimed at; development of mind and morals and manners together into strong and symmetrical manhood. His students were moulded by his own strong Christian character, and the devout simplicity and confidence with which he taught all truth from the stand of Christian theism. Not as a sectarian, not as a religious enthusiast, such as Dr. Griffin, his predecessor, had been, but with a sweet reasonableness and a magnetism never surpassed, he presented belief in God as the true philosophy of life and of the world. This, we are told, was the secret of his wonderful character-moulding power.

"The question is not," writes President Porter, of Yale, "whether the college shall or shall not teach theology, but *what* theology shall it teach—theology according to Comte and Spencer, or according to Bacon and Christ? Theology according to Moses and Paul or according to Buckle and Draper? For a college to hesitate to teach theism and Christianity is practically to proclaim that in the opinions of its guardians the evidence for and against is so evenly balanced that it would be unfair for them to throw the weight of their influence on either side and is in fact to throw it on the side of materialism, fatalism and atheism."

Here is the reason why we, as Christians, demand institutions of higher learning dominated by Christian truth. Not to do so is to surrender our youth to materialism and agnosticism.

"The end of education," says Jean Paul Richter, "is to elevate above the spirit of the age." Commenting on this President Payne, of the Ohio Wesleyan, remarks:

"Richter says, 'The end of education is to elevate above the spirit of the age.' That is a great truth which, amid the clamor about an education of the times and for the times, we do well to heed. We must have a culture which ennobles, enlarges and enriches the mind and lifts it out of the materialistic atmosphere of the age. Hence the necessity of a judicious attention to the classics, ancient and modern, to literature, to history and philosophy and kindred studies.

"We cannot afford to strike at genuine culture or at Christian faith, and become the abettors of a demoralizing materialism, in order to make our educational work conform to the demands of a false public sentiment."

What the world wants to-day above all other wants is men and women of lofty type and genuine character and masterful power,—men and women whose souls as well as brains have been quickened, who perceive that intellectual good is empty and worthless, a positive curse to the world, unless underneath it there be a good heart, who perceive that culture, apart from faith in God and devotion to man, have a tendency to produce an artificial and unsympathetic character and who therefore have the Man of Galilee for their ideal.

It is asserted in some quarters that the spirit of materialism and rationalism which characterizes the age has entered even our Christian colleges and universities. It startles us to read in Mr. Thwing's Treatise on American colleges the statement: "The American college has ceased to be in its government and organization and instruction a distinctively religious force. "

Dr. J. W. Mendenhall in the *Christian Advocate* (June 6, 1889) declares with a startling array of substantiating facts, that as in Germany, France, Holland, England, so here rationalism has its headquarters in the colleges. He specifically charges that Yale is the center of American rationalism and Harvard intensely rationalistic. If this is indeed true it is a lamentable departure from the original intention of the founders of those institutions. Harvard bears the name of a Congregational minister and carries on its seal the motto " *Christo et Ecclesiæ.* " Yale was planted to be the foundation of even a stricter orthodoxy than was taught at Harvard.

I am constrained to receive these statements with some allowance. The statistics show that whereas there was but one Christian student in ten at Harvard in 1853, in 1890 the proportion was one in five. Other Christian colleges show the same improvement. Mr. Thwing himself says that about one-half of the students in our colleges are professing Christians. Dr. Dorchester also calls attention to the encouraging fact that religious revivals are of more frequent occurrence and that almost every institution now has a Y. M. C. A. organization within its ranks.

Yet we must not be blind to facts. The spirit of the age is materialistic. The magic word of the day is science, and " science, " says Prof. Diman, " discusses force and method but says nothing of God, freedom and immortality. She leads us, therefore, to the tree of knowledge but not to the tree of life." "When history is reduced to the rigid and inexorable laws of physical science, as it is by Buckle and Goldwin Smith, and moral philosophy is based on molecular movements, as it is in substance by Spencer and Bain; when the data of ethics must be searched for only among the rubbish of matter, with its necessitarian laws, these studies lose their inspiring and ennobling power. It would be perilous to turn our American youth into these sterile pastures to herd with the cattle and to feed on that which perishes alike with themselves."

These words remind us of the question Bishop Spaulding asks in his address on Ideals: "Is the material progress of the nineteenth century a cradle or a grave? Are we to continue to dig and delve and peer into matter until God and the soul fade from our view and we become like the things we work in?"

Against such a degradation of the glory of our age; against such a prostitution of science, which DuBois Raymond declares owes its origin to Christianity; against such a humiliation and destruction of the soul of man, it is the mission of the Christian colleges of America to contend.

And this they can only do by making the colleges a center of moral power and Christian influence. John Calet placed the image of the Child Jesus over the master's chair in the German school beside St. Paul's, London, and engraved beneath it the words, "Hear Ye Him." The same ideal and the same motto should be found in all our institutions of learning. Jesus Christ furnishes us not only the picture of a complete and perfect character, but his unfolding youth furnishes us with the ideal of character development. We find it compressed into one verse: "And Jesus increased in wisdom and stature and in favor with God and man." Here are the four lines along which there must be growth if the youth is to receive a symmetrical and well-balanced development. "In stature"—a physical development; "in wisdom"—a mental training and discipline which shall draw out (*educo*) the faculties of the mind and give the young the power to grapple with the problems of life; in "the favor of God"—spiritual development through that communion of the soul with the Infinite Spirit which quickens all the spiritual forces within, irradiating character with the "beauty of the Lord" and clothing it with a power that is not born of earth; finally, growth in favor of man—or social development—the knowledge of the world, of human nature, of the requirements of social intercourse; the refinement of manners and address in meeting men which constitutes such an invaluable addition to the character of the young man or woman when they step forth into the world.

This is symmetrical development, physical, mental, spiritual, social; and Jesus Christ is the ideal whom it is our privilege to set before the youth of our land. He is the *only* ideal, and the master who does not point to Him saying "*Hear Ye Him*," will fail of his mission, no matter how brilliant an instructor.

The vast majority of the colleges of this land have been founded as we have seen, for the avowed purpose of exalting Christ in the culture of our land. · To Christ they must remain true or lose their power and their glory. "Not until this republic has made a nearer approach to its decline and fall," says President Payne, "will infidel schools or schools

REV. JONATHAN BLANCHARD, D. D.

antagonistic to Christianity, rise to commanding influence." On the contrary, the more of the teachings and spirit of the Great Teacher all our educational institutions inculcate and stamp upon the characters of their students, the wider will be their influence."

To live for common ends is to be common. The highest faith makes still the highest man. For we grow like the things our souls believe, and rise or sink as we aim high or low. No mirror shows such likeness of the face as faith we live by, of the heart and mind. We are, in very truth, that which we love, and love, like the noblest deeds, is born of faith.

We most sincerely hope and pray that this institution founded by Christian faith and sustained through many a trying hour, may ever be true to this high ideal, giving to the youth who enter her halls that symmetrical Christian culture which will fit them for noble life, useful citizenship and the eternal blessedness of those who not through knowledge alone, but through character, are fit for fellowship with God.

The Chairman: And now let me introduce to you another neighbor, one whom we see for the first time, but whom, once heard, we shall wish to hear again, and often, the Rev. C. W. Hiatt, pastor of the First Congregational Church of Peoria. His theme is

"THE CHURCH AND THE COLLEGE."

Mr. Chairman, Ladies and Gentlemen:

Wholly in addition to the special and agreeable mission of congratulation which brings me here, I am personally conscious of an interest in this institution, in which are commingled the elements of curiosity and gratitude. I am curious to know what meat the oratorical Cæsars of Knox have been eating for the past few years, to make them so great and so terrible in the eyes of college men. I am grateful, because, in-directly, this college has influenced my own career by calling into educational work, more than forty years ago, the great and inspiring man, under whom it was my fortune to receive the academic tutelage. A man, who brought to the prairies of Illinois somewhat of the granite of his own New England hills, who never suffered a pupil to pass beyond his care without receiving the impression of his own heroic soul, the man who wrote your college diploma, graduating thirteen classes here, the second president of Knox, and the first president of Wheaton, Jonathan Blanchard.

I think that we more than pay a tribute to the past to-day. We gather an inspiration for ourselves. When that veracious and emotional traveler, Mark Twain, was in Palestine, he ran across the grave of Adam. He thereupon lifted up his voice and wept, for he recognized in him a distant relative. It was his way of paying respects to the class of people who are always raking over the ashes of the past, and clothing every cindered relic with a sacred sentiment. The Innocent, however, would scarcely have turned his ridicule upon a scene like this. If America has anything on which to pride herself, it is the memory of those devoted spirits,.who, fifty years and more ago, at great sacrifice, planted in the beech and oak clearings of Ohio and Michigan, and amid the prairie grasses of Illinois and Iowa, the foundations of colleges, wherein learning should ever be the hand-maiden of religion, and where the privileges of education should never be restricted, whether on account of race, or sect, or sex. Such, I believe, was the genesis of the institution whose foundation we celebrate. These men sought a perfect state of society. They decried and discarded all patent processes of human restoration and development. They looked for the perfect state of society to come of perfecting its unit, the individual man. This would be accomplished by developing what was noblest in him, the intellect and heart, giving to him both knowledge and faith, whose highest exponents were the college and the church. These two must work together.

It was a good philosophy. There is a natural correlation between the institution that lifts the flambeau of truth, and the institution that lights the torches of love. You cannot illuminate the world with either one alone. Jesus was the "truth." God is " love" and when these two met in Christ, who was both God and man, love and truth, he it was who could justly and triumphantly declare "I am the light of the world." Truth and love are weak when unrelated. Truth becomes a pale and sickly glimmer. Love becomes a vapid sentimentalism, guilty of absurdities and extremes. But when love and truth unite, the dark earth becomes ablaze with light. Then it is that Oberlin forsakes his Strasburg for the mountains of the Vosges, and Mackay turns his back on universities of Britain to hide away in the consecrated smithy of interior Africa, and Chalmers descends from the loftiest pulpit in Christendom to bury himself in the lowly parish of St. John's. It is when truth and love unite that upon the iniquities of the earth there comes the expulsive power. It is intelligent Christianity and Christianized intelligence that will give the smile to the desert, and to the wilderness a rose. And these are the product of the college and the church when unitedly at work. It is a divine relation, and what God hath joined together let no man put asunder.

But this was not a new philosophy. The Puritan, whether of the Mayflower or later immigration, built his two cabins side by side, one for religion and one for education. In the planting of all the noble institutions of those early times, Harvard, Yale, Princeton, The College of William and Mary, the purpose, written or unwritten, was for " Christ and His Church." It is a significant fact that when the 260 volumes of John Harvard all perished in the flames but one, the title of this one was " The Christian Warfare Against the Devil." In this connection it is proper to inquire what is .the relation of colleges and churches in our day. It is clear enough that the churches are not contributing their produce as the fathers did, peas, corn and beans, to the support of these institutions. For instance, in Illinois there are 304 churches in the order to which I belong. Of this number 215 gave nothing for education last year. And yet there is a relation between the church and college. We observe a day of prayer for colleges once a year—that is a part of the day, and part of it, a very small portion of the day we pray for you, brethren, but in no part of the day do we *pay* for you. We send a few of our boys and girls to school. However they do not all go to the Christian college in the vicinage. A while ago in a church of five hundred members, I noticed that fourteen young men and maidens went out of town to school. Of this number four traveled a thousand miles, three five hundred miles, three went into a neighboring state, two attended the state university, which, to say the least, did not prepare young men for the ministry, while two of the fourteen, went forty miles to the Christian college, which had a right to claim the entire fourteen. It was a well-appointed institution. It was thriving excepting that it lacked pupils and finances. All this was wrong. The church associations sometimes send a committee to inspect the college. These visitors appear for a day, returning with interest the vacant stare of the Greek and Latin on the blackboards, walking wearily through the scientific halls, and spending their last hour looking at the backs of the books in the library; and when next the association meets they report that the college is doing well, and recommend that it be given the same sympathy in the future as in the past.

Surely the relation of church and college might be closer and more practical. For instance I do not like to have our boys going to Harvard

and our girls going to Vassar, with a noble Christian college open to both
at our very door. Speaking of Vassar reminds me of a little parody
that went the rounds when I was editor of a quite meritorious but not
financially successful college journal—

> "There was a young maiden of Vassar,
> In drawing no one could surpass her,
> She drew like Lorain—a very long train,
> And a check that astonished the cashier."

Some people, however, have a deep-seated prejudice against co-educational schools. A graduate of Yale once asked "Is it true that students
of co-educational colleges go out paired?" And the reply came laconi-
cally "Yes, *pre-pared.*" The churches must sustain these Christian
schools—Christian enough to educate both boys and girls.

It rests upon a reasonable proposition. The churches expect the
colleges to fill their pulpits. The colleges have a right, therefore to ask
the churches to fill their class-rooms and treasuries. I do not believe
that we shall absolve ourselves of obligation by passing around the con-
tribution boxes once a year. Often such collections only just suffice to
fill the cup of despair. But this I maintain, while we are appointing
committees to attend to the educational interests of the black man and
the red man and the yellow man and the brown man, we should also ap-
point a committee to take care of the white man who is so unfortunate
as to be born in the United States. A committee that shall not only
secure funds but also pupils for the neighboring Christian college. It is
a theory of mine that when pupils throng a school it is easier to secure
money than when financial agents throng the rich man's door. I count
it among the privileges of Christian ministry to encourage the holy
grace of intellectual discontent in young men and women until they resolutely set their faces for a liberal education, thus seeking to add to
their faith that knowledge which shall clothe it with all but irresistible
power. The minister is not usually oppressed with an overplus of funds.
He often laments that he may not pay the way of aspirant boys and girls,
but perhaps he has the commission only to pave the way. I have
thought that it would be good for colleges to adopt a heroic plan of giving absolutely free tuition to such young men as ministers may recomend.
For I am convinced that where the churches have their treasures there
their hearts will also be.

Undoubtedly the battle plain of truth and error in the next one
hundred years will be this American continent and perhaps this very

Mississippi valley. The mighty agents of the truth, the pledge of victory, will be the joint product of our churches and our schools. It therefore behooves the church and college to co-operate. Let the pulpit lift the clarion of inspiration. Let the pew pour out its wealth. Let the college open wide its doors!

A chorus of college boys here sang Founders' Day Song to the tune, " John Brown's Body," the body of students joining in the last refrain. The song was composed by Prof. L. S. Pratt.

To sing the praise of dear old Knox we bid you now prepare,
For those who love these college walls have lately been aware,
Within the last six months or so, there's something in the air
    Which augurs well for Knox.

REFRAIN:—   Money has begun to flow,
    Alumni hope is in a glow,
    Students have increased, and so
        All augurs well for Knox.

The history of our college home has always been our pride,
For head and heart and spirit there are cultured side by side.
Success has our alumni crowned in everything they've tried,
    'Tis the history of our Knox.

REFRAIN:—   Success in church and school and state,—
    Knox blood has always made men great,
    And so her past we celebrate,
        Grand history of old Knox.

So forward is our thought to-day: we look toward coming years.
Our hopes are bright: new eras dawn: the darkness disappears.
A prospect of the future day with joy our bosom cheers,—
    The future of new Knox.

REFRAIN:—   Our past but faintly typifies
    Success on-looking hope descries,—
    O! vision sweet to longing eyes.
        Rare future! noble Knox.

And so with loving loyalty we offer heart and hand
Anew to thee to-day, dear Knox, thy stalwart student band,
And pledge to do our best for thee, whatever thy command,
    Our best for thee, old Knox.

REFRAIN:—   Knox carissima! our own!
                   To the breeze thy banner's thrown!
                   Love to thee, and thee alone,
                        We pledge to-day, dear Knox.

REFRAIN, REPEATED:—
                   Zip, rah, boom, rah, Knox, Knox, Knox!
                   Zip, rah, boom, rah, rocks, rocks, rocks!
                   Zip, rah, boom, rah, welcome, new epochs!
                   Boom, rah, Knox, *Knox*, KNOX!

The Chairman: We are honored in the presence this morning of
a man affectionately called by his thousands of friends up and down
this country as "Father Coffin." He is himself a founder of a great
order and a strong ally and friend of the workingmen, especially those
whose lives are spent in the employ of the railway corporations, though
he is himself a farmer. I have the pleasure of introducing the Hon. L.
S. Coffin. The subject to which he will speak is

"THE VALUE OF A COLLEGE EDUCATION."

Mr. Chairman, Ladies and Gentlemen:

Why a humble man—a farmer— a man who never enjoyed the inestimable privilege of such institutions as this whose anniversary we celebrate to-day should be invited to participate in these commendable festiv-
ities, I cannot conceive, unless it be upon the principle which underlies
that immortal and precious sonnet, "Home, Sweet Home." I think I
have been told that the writer of that song never knew what the joys
of home were, that he was a homeless wanderer. He knew its value by
its loss or absence. This great honor conferred upon me by being
invited to take some little part upon this platform, at this interesting
time, adds a keenness to the pang of the ever returning regret that I am
not and cannot ever be reckoned among the alumni of any college or
university. I was thoughtlessly robbed of boyhood opportunities for
education and when a young man my services were too valuable as a
worker on the farm to allow of academic privileges. When of age I
found myself so lacking in all discipline and culture that I was forced to
make some effort for an education. But the extent of my schooling
was not more than about two years in the preparatory department at
Oberlin, Ohio, whither I came drawn by the report of its wonderful facilities offered to young men. I am by birth and life-long

work a farmer, and my life has been one of such close confinement to toil and public work in God's providence laid upon me, that I have never been able to command enough time to devote to reading, even so as to be at all at home with intelligent, cultured men. Strange as it may seem, with all this lack of education and training, it has been my lot in the past thirty days to stand frequently before public audiences, as here to-day, and all these years I have been compelled to reap the harvest from seeds sown in early life. Being extremely sensitive of my lack, I have never yet been able to rise before a public audience to speak without humiliating embarrassment. I thus humble myself before you to-day, and violate all rules of public speaking in thus opening to your view my life in order to enforce what I would say to every young man and boy, young woman and girl who has the ambition for an education, to let no obstacle stand between you and a thorough course of study. With the opportunities now at the hands of every young man and woman it becomes almost the unpardonable sin not to secure a good education.

But I am expected to speak to you a few minutes upon the subject of a liberal education as connected with labor and the efforts of labor to better its own condition. It is not necessary for me to say here that my whole soul is in hearty sympathy with labor. All my life I have been a hard working man in the manual labor of the farm. I have seen, of course, as the years have come and gone, all the labor orders come into existence. I do not say I have always agreed with all the movements made, or the motives that have actuated some of these orders; still, underneath or behind them all, or nearly all, is this grand motive, viz.: the betterment of the condition of the laboring man and his family. Some of the ways and means to this end adopted by some, I may not approve, but it is not necessary at this time and place to dwell upon the errors of labor. We are here to point, if possible, to avenues that lead out, up and away from not only the errors, but the woes, the burdens, and if I may say it, the un-American distinctions that class one set of men as laborers and another as capitalists. I look with dread, and I may say sorrow and alarm, at this increasing use of the word "class" or "classes" as applied to the American people. The intelligent, honest laboring man is the true "American." If there must be any distinctions made aside from that of honest manhood as against meanness and knavery, let it be that of intelligence as against ignorance. Any distinction based on wealth and poverty should have no place in this land of equality. Any distinction of this nature I hope will always be as now, based upon a very unstable foundation. May the time never come in this land when the son of the laborer of to-day cannot be the father of the millionaire to-morrow. But the question is, how shall this condition of things be restrained by us in this land of freedom and equal rights? The answer comes short and quick—viz.: by maintaining and consecrating just such institutions as these to the lifting up of the children of the men of toil.

Labor is impatient, is impulsive. What it wants, it thinks it wants badly and wants it now. It does not read history, or, if it reads, it does not always heed its lessons. God is always at the helm of the ship that carries all humanity. A thousand years are as one day with Him. Moses had to lead his laborers for two hundred years through the wilderness ways before he gained what they struck for. They needed discipline. They needed education and God gave them time to get it. Labor must look along the years and work and wait. The father laborer of to-day may, like Moses, only see the promised land from the mountain top and in joyful faith and anticipation see the glorious land of life his educated children are sure to have. There is not a class of men on earth who have a greater interest at stake in the establishment, maintenance and patronage of such schools as this and of our common public schools than do the laboring men of this country. Here is their only hope. The parent, who is a parent, looks not so much to his own as to his child's good. Take the children of the average railroad man. They inherit from the cool-headed, determined, brave, energetic, keen, discriminating, strong-hearted man, a make-up that can be likened to a steam engine. My observation is that these children, as a rule, are superior in many respects to the ordinary child. Such children, educated, become the leaders of men. Instead of brakemen, conductors, engineers, they become superintendents, managers, presidents, directors, capitalists, or if inclined to other pursuits, merchants, lawyers, and influential men and women. They go to the top. But if neglected, not educated, they drift along in the ruts their fathers made and class labor becomes entailed with all its degrading consequences. If I should bring any objection to these labor orders it would be that when one once enters a brotherhood there is danger of a feeling something like this: "Well, I am a brotherhood man now and it is a pretty good thing. I like the boys and I will stay with them." The ambition to go up higher, I have sometimes thought, seems in a measure smothered. All these orders should, like the various churches, be considered not as an end, but as a means to a higher end—to develop the best there is in a man and to unite the powers of the many in overcoming wrong and establishing right; to draw in and lift up the weak and those in danger and need. I have, as most know, a great interest in the Brotherhood of Trainmen, whose headquarters are in your city, but I should feel sad to think that any one of them should feel that once a brakeman always a brakeman, or that once an employee always an employee. I should like the time to come when each one of these men shall be his own employer; have a business of his own, be his own master. But if he cannot be that I do want him to see to it that his children shall receive the benefits of such institutions as this, so that they may forge their way to the front, and that, too, in time to take to their better homes and surroundings the parents who have made it possible, by their self-denial, for them to get an education. I would not be too severe but I do candidly, firmly believe, that no healthy, honest, temperate, economical laboring man, with a wife who is a helpmeet for him, can have any real excuse for not lifting himself and his posterity to a higher social plane through the power and influence that will come by the education of his children. The great drawback, the great drain upon the wages of labor heretofore has been the enormous drain upon these wages for drink and tobacco. Give me the money spent yearly for these worse than useless things and I will put through college every child of labor in America. There is no hope for the children of the laboring man so long as the saloon divides his wages between his family and itself. This fact, thank God, the railroad man has begun to see. If all classes of toilers would do as these railroad men are now doing, we should soon see these educational halls crowded with the children from the families whose only capital at present is brawn but which in the next generation will be both brawn and brain. God speed the day when the schools like this will have to be multiplied to meet the growing wants of labor. .

The Chairman: You know that some have read the future of the small college in the fate that befell the seven fat kine, which, in Pharaoh's dream fed in the meadows of Egypt, the fate of being eaten up by the lean and hungry universities. But I do not fear such a fate for Knox, for you see I have invited one of the representatives of the great university up on the lake shore into our fields. I have the honor and pleasure of introducing him as our friend, Dr. Albion W. Small, of the University of Chicago. He will speak of

"THE UNIVERSITY AND THE COLLEGE."*

Ladies and Gentlemen:

It is a great pleasure as well as an honor to extend to Knox College a most hearty greeting on behalf of the University of Chicago. I rejoice that I live in a generation in which it is possible for the members of Christian institutions to behave toward each other as gentlemen should. The age of ungentlemanly, unchristian, deadly rivalry between institutions of learning is happily passing if not past. We are getting to see that the prosperity of one is the prosperity of all. We have at Chicago the heartiest sympathy for Knox, because we are so much alike in our situation—we are both poor. Poverty is a relative matter after all. Poverty is assets just a dollar short of liabilities. Poverty is legs a trifle too long for the pantaloons. Coming down in the train, President Harper and I were looking over the University budget for next year, and it appears that if we cannot retrench, our expenditure next year will be forty thousand dollars more than our receipts.

The first suggestion that I will urge with reference to the college is that its mission is not primarily literary culture; it is the maturing and strengthening of character, in which the training and finish of mind is only one element. You remember the story of Count Von Moltke, Prussia's great field-marshal in the Franco-Prussian war. When his aide entered his room at night, and said, "War is declared," the old field-marshal simply pointed to the second portfolio on the shelf. The war was already fought in anticipation. It is a proud career to be able to stand before young students and to help them anticipate the battle of life. The first mission of the college, the fundamental mission, is the maturing of character. Between fourteen and twenty is the period when ambitions are formed, and it is in that period that the college has its first function of instructing manhood. The man whose teaching I enjoyed most in college, left upon me this one impression, which I can remember definitely—I happened to fall in with him one day walking down College Street. He commenced talking to me, and this is the one remark which remained with me: "It is best not to let one moment of time go to waste." He suggested that when I was waiting for my dinner at my boarding house, I should have something light to read which I did not care to take up more valuable time for, and it was during the

* *Dr. Small was not able to reproduce his remarks in full and they are published from partial stenographic notes taken by a gentleman in the audience.*

few moments each day while waiting for dinner, that I read whatever I have of Dickens. From my fifth to my fourteenth year I was in a Sunday School in which through all that time there was one superintendent. The only words from that man's lips that I can remember to-day are words which he uttered one Saturday afternoon when I was blacking a pair of boots, and he said to me: "Do you always black the heels as well as you do the toes?" That was all he said, but I thought of his remarks afterwards, and his words stayed with me. The keenest disappointment of my life was in 1876, when I made application for a position as instructor at Knox College, and received a reply from the president that if my application had been received twenty-four hours earlier it would probably have obtained a favorable answer. Up to date it is actually the keenest disappointment I have ever suffered. The disappointment of that day in 1876 has been revived during this hour when I have learned more than I knew before of what Knox College actually was and is for the education of a boy. I would give more for the ideals, the purposes of the men and women whose lives have gone into the structure of this college than for all the libraries that wealth can buy.

The second mission of the college, and after all it is the second mission, not the first, is the distribution to students of the sum of knowledge acquired up to date. The college is to the university the station on the pipe line, of which the university may be called the main. It is the work of the specialist to learn the last returns from the front. The business of the college is to put into the minds of the students the latest contents of the book of nature that any one has reported. It is often spoken of as a misfortune if a boy or girl is obliged to get a college education in a small college. I have had experience both in small colleges and in great universities, and it seems to me exactly the reverse. The best opportunities for the maturing of character during these forming years are not in connection with the great universities; they are in the comparative seclusion of the small college, where the students meet intimately and freely the men who are above them in intellect. The small college is the place to get the foundation of knowledge. The association of the small college is the world in which the work of the public school is best continued. I think we are never so sure of entertaining angels unawares as when we harbor in a town a body of young men engaged in the pursuits of education. Reference has been made to the rationalism of our American and European universities. The difference between the typical university man and the typical college man is the difference between the outlook in the bow, and the passenger resting securely in the cabin below. The business of the university is this general rationalism which does not cut away from faith any more than Columbus cut away from the theory of gravitation when he sailed from Palos. The best diviners of truth are not those people who frown upon scepticism. The place for the foundation work, the safe place, the right place, is not with the sceptic. Hence the atmosphere of the college, rather than the university, is preferable for the young student. But it is not right of those who want this work done to denounce the reasonable sceptics, *i. e.* the scientific searchers for new truth. They are sceptics with faith in their heart,· with new discoveries and imaginations before their eyes.

You know the old story of the school master in England who has a monument in Westminster Abbey. . The facts are these as related by tradition: It was the custom of the teacher to wear his cap when teaching the school. One day the king entered, but the master did not remove his hat. When the pupils went out, the teacher uncovered his head. The king asked, "Why do you take off your cap now?" The pedagogue replied: "Because it would not do for the boys to know that there is any greater man in England than the master." The growth of universities has not diminished but rather increased the responsibility of colleges. It is the right of any college which, like Knox, is fulfilling its proper function, to claim a dignity which makes it essentially the peer of any educational institution of any grade.

The Chairman: We have heard much of the past of Knox College and now we shall hear before closing these interesting exercises a brief forecast of the future, and our prophet is one who has helped as much as any one person to make the past and the present of this college to build an enduring foundation for a great future. I introduce him who needs no introduction, the teacher of thousands in the forty-three years of his connection with Knox College, Professor Albert Hurd.

THE FUTURE OF KNOX COLLEGE.

Ladies and Gentlemen:

I am neither a prophet nor the son of a prophet, but perhaps I can make good the prediction just uttered by President Finley that the last speech will be a short one. When a single Professor of Divinity with three learned companions left the Monastery of Croyland for Cambridge in England, and hired a barn in which to receive the young men who came to them to receive instruction, they could not look very far into the future. They were called of God to do a noble work; in faith they obeyed the call and entered upon their mission. Centuries have rolled away since that time and we can now see the result, but the founders of the great university could not foresee the coming Chaucer and Milton, and Bacon, and Macaulay. In like manner when a few learned men commenced a course of lectures at Oxford, the future greatness of their school was not discerned; even the eye of faith must have fallen far short of revealing the glorious history concealed by the veil of years yet to come. Wickliffe and Wolsey, Wesley and Whitefield, Lyell and Gladstone, with their commanding influence upon human affairs and human destiny, could not have been anticipated. And so it cannot now be seen what mighty and influential minds are hereafter to be discovered and trained within the walls of Knox College; what perennial streams of fertility and gladness are to flow for many centuries from this infant seat of learning. Her self-sacrificing founders came to these prairies in the same spirit which moved Abraham to leave his Mesopotamian home. They came here scarcely knowing whither they came, dwelling in tabernacles and looking for a city of which God should be the builder. They organized a Christian college and planted a Christian church. Fifty years have come and gone and from the results we may form some conception of what the future has in store. Knox college has already furnished at least six college presidents, twenty college professors, a hundred ministers of the gospel and missionaries, eighty lawyers, forty physicians and twenty journalists and editors. Our graduates are found as judges in our higher and lower courts; they are an army of superintendents and teachers in our public schools; they are successful business men and farmers; and many not included in these lists are doing valuable work for the country and for humanity. Where has their work been done? They are in our own cities and villages from the Atlantic to the Pacific; they have gone to Europe and to Africa, to Australia and to Japan, and everywhere are doing noble service for God and for the highest interests of their fellowmen. Knox College has given these men and women the opportunity and the means of preparing themselves for the work of life, and by the efficient work they have performed has made good her right to a continued existence. What Knox College has done in the past day of small things she will certainly do on a much larger scale in the near future, if only it be possible to place the great boon of a liberal education within the reach of the constantly increasing number of enterprising and ambitious youth who may come here for guidance and instruction. As Galesburg enlarges and improves; as the country develops, our college must increase her endowment and her ability to give a thorough and complete education or her day of usefulness will be short. In many directions enlargement is needed, but in none is a radical change more imperative than in the department of natural science, and it is to be earnestly desired that the means of erecting a science hall and of equipping it for such work in science as the times demand, will soon be provided. Should the present attempt to raise $200,000 be crowned with success and should Dr. Pearsons' gift of $50,-000 be secured, a new era of prosperity will surely come, vindicating the wisdom and realizing the hopes of the founders of Knox College, whose memory we to-day so auspiciously celebrate.

After this address all joined in singing "Founders' Day Hymn," composed by Prof. L. S. Pratt, and sung to the tune of "America":

> Our Fathers' God! to-day
> Grateful to Thee we pray,
>   Before Thee bow:
> As Thou hast led of old,
> With mercies manifold,
> Still by Thy love enfold
>   Thy children now.
>
> By Thine own spirit fired,
> By heavenly love inspired,
>   Our fathers came
> Into this prairie land:—
> O, toil with heart and hand!
> O, gain of harvests grand!
>   In God's great name.
>
> Guide Thou this college still!
> May we the hopes fulfil
>   Of founders true.
> O, keep us in Thy fear!
> May truth be ever dear,
> And God's love shine more clear
>   Each year anew.

The benediction was then pronounced by the Rev. E. G. Smith, of Princeton, Ill., a member of the first class, 1846.

EVENING EXERCISES.

PRESIDENT FINLEY: I have the pleasure and the honor of introducing as the chairman of the evening our distinguished townsman, whom we are all glad to welcome back to Galesburg, after his years of honorable service abroad, and whom the College is especially glad to have in its council again, the Honorable Clark E. Carr, our recent Minister to Denmark.

INTRODUCTORY ADDRESS

BY THE HON. CLARK E. CARR.

The orator who is to address us this evening is bound to the people of Galesburg by bands of steel. When (after a line for the great Santa Fe railroad ten miles away from our city had been nearly settled upon) I went to Topeka and called upon him and other general officers of the company, I found in him a friend who favored us, and he had great influence in having the line finally established through this city.

It is a frequent expression with him that he loves to talk to old soldiers and to young men. He is fond of speaking to old soldiers for they are his comrades. In his early youth he was a brave and faithful Union soldier. When the war was over he chose the profession of the law, to which he has steadfastly devoted himself, and which he would not abandon for a seat in the United States Senate, which was offered him. Notwithstanding the exactions of his profession, he has found time for literary pursuits outside of it, communion with the great and the wise and the learned. It is his opinion that men in every profession and trade and occupation, however humble, may bask in the sunshine of intellectual culture, and he therefore loves to speak to young men of the splendors that are open before them, and the felicities to which they may attain.

Only those fully appreciate him who know him well enough to meet him socially, when he is able to throw off the cares of his profession and admit them to partake of the bounties of the rich stores of knowledge he has garnered, and to revel with him in the eloquence and poetry and art of all the ages. He will this evening give us glimpses of the *Kingdom of Light* in which he lives.

I have the honor of presenting to you Colonel George R. Peck, General Solicitor of the Santa Fe Railway Company.

ADDRESS.

BY THE HON. GEORGE R. PECK.

Mr. Chairman, Ladies and Gentlemen:

I appreciate most highly the kind expressions of Colonel Carr in presenting me to you, although I realize that they are prompted rather by the friendly relations which have existed between us for many years, than by any merit of my own.

My subject for to-night, as has been announced, is

THE KINGDOM OF LIGHT.

Somewhere in the depths of every heart there is a spring which answers to the touch of memory. A strain of music that you heard in childhood has a peculiar indefinable sweetness which others do not perceive. And *days* have their significance; for each and all have chronicled births and deaths, and have been filled with the joys and sorrows that make up human life. In Kinglake's " Invasion of the Crimea" there is a beautiful chapter on the mystery of holy shrines, which tells how out of sentiment of love for the holy sepulchre, and of rivalry for the possession of that sacred place, great nations drifted into war, and armies sailed to far-off lands, making days that had been common, memorable forevermore, and consecrating new shrines for future pilgrimages. It is not, I think, a mere instinct of worldly wisdom that inspires the reverence which men feel for historic days and places. It is human nature reaching out unconsciously, and with a wisdom which it does not comprehend, for that which is ideally good and beautiful. The birthday of Abraham Lincoln is, by the laws of Illinois, a legal holiday. But it was something higher than a state legislature which set it apart and made it a day for joy and pride, for high resolves and for a new faith in the United States of America. Knox College counts this as its birthday; and I think it was an extremely happy thought which prompted the authorities to give it the place of dignity in the calendar of its history. It is no longer young, and, I doubt not, it is already beginning to feel the influence which is, perhaps, the best part of the life of an educational institution—the unseen, silent power of the accumulated years. I do not wonder that students of Oxford and Cambridge, of Harvard, Yale and Princeton feel a thrill of pride when the great names in their annals are spoken; and this college does a wise thing when it gives itself a voice to tell of what it has done and what, if it please God, it will do. A life that has no romance in it is hardly worth the living, and a college which contains nothing in its history that appeals to the imagination is, to say the least, lacking in a most essential element of usefulness. But you have it to overflowing. I know of no story more full of romantic interest than that of the founding of Knox College. I do not speak of the official or legislative organization, for that was merely the formal record of what had already been thought out. February 15 is Founders' Day, because on that day the act of incorporation was passed. But there was a foundation under the foundation, even as DeQuincey speaks of the depths that are below the depths. Before the Legislature made Knox College a body corporate, its walls had been reared in the mind of its founder. What dreams of the future came to him in those early days before the colonists set their faces to the west, we know not! But the college with all its possibilities was already upbuilded, massive, permanent and beautiful, before hammer or trowel had rung, or the silence had been broken by the voice of the artisan. It seems like that wonderful vision of Coleridge:

"In Xanadu did Kubla Khan
A stately pleasure dome decree."

I should like to know what hint it was, what suggestion or thought came into the mind of George W. Gale and inspired him to the enterprise that to-day counts as its accomplished result this great college and this beautiful city. It must have looked quixotic, a wild, impossible scheme, to plant a college in the wilderness and to expect the city to grow up around it. But it did. The college and the city have lovingly walked hand in hand, each counting the other the apple of its eye.

To-night you are thinking of the past. You are glad and proud, too, for what Knox College has done. It has seen good and evil days; prosperity and adversity have entered its doors, but this birthday is a happy one and the omens point joyously to the future. But I must remind you that self-congratulation, while it has its uses, cannot keep an educational institution prosperous. The patrons and friends, the officers and faculty of the college, would be worthless if results did not come to the full measure of their effort. No college ever amounted to anything that was kept alive just for the sake of being called a college. It must *do*. There is nothing of value in it if it cannot point to higher character, to truer lives, to better things made possible by its effort.

It is a fortunate thing for this institution that it is located in a region to which Nature has given her kindliest smiles; a land of meadows and of gardens and of goodly people living in goodly homes. I cannot help thinking that the subtle law of heredity has played a powerful part in the success which has hitherto attended the work of Knox College. The parental type is transmitted from generation to generation, and the iron which was in the blood of the pioneers gives tone and vigor to the students of to-day. What Knox College will do in the future depends upon the character of the teachers and instructors who fill the chairs; but after all, the students themselves must set the mark of the institution. The most skillful baker fails when the flour is poor. If students ask what a college can do for them the true answer is: It can do for them only what they do for *it* in its good name and character as an institution of learning. A college and its students are trustees for each other. They give and take and each is richer by the process. I cannot recall truer words than those once spoken by a great president of Harvard who said to his students: "It is a superficial view of things which leads to the distinction between education and self-education. In point of fact all education is self-education, the only difference being that education in churches and schools and colleges, and amidst librairies, museums and laboratories, is self-education under the best advantages." To the learners, and not to the teachers, I feel that what I have to say ought to be directed.

A man of mature years can find no happier occasion than that which permits him to stand face to face with young and ardent searchers after knowledge. The student is always an object of interest. His presence is an inspiration, and his face an open book on which are written a hope and a prophecy. This occasion, young ladies and gentlemen, commemorative of the great work of the founder of this college, is a fitting time for laying the foundation of a noble career. The scholar, if he be worthy to wear the name, hears every day a call to be consecrated, feels in every hour the baptism of a higher life.

It would, perhaps, be more in harmony with the times, if I should speak to you on some theme of immediate and pressing importance. Such themes there are; and I beg of you to believe it is not because I underestimate them that I have chosen to ask you to rest for a little while in a serener air. The hungry problems of to-day will have their hearing without asking permission of you or me. The age is restless; it is self-assertive; it is pleased with the sound of its own voice and confident in the strength of its own arm. And yet in its heart there is a profound sorrow. When men turn their minds persistently to social and economic questions; when labor is dissatisfied and capital alarmed; when the prices of food and the mystery of supply and demand occupy their thoughts by night and by day, we may be sure that something is out of place in the machinery we call civilization.

But of these things it is not my purpose to speak. I allude to them because, as it seems to me, every true heart must be deeply sensible of their importance and must constantly feel how dark a shadow they cast on sad and discontented lives. But this hour is dedicated to the young, the ambitious, the joyous and the generous; and so I shall ask you to another field, where, perhaps, we can gather some hints, which shall also be helps, for the journey upon which you have entered.

You do not, I presume, call yourselves philosophers, but you are probably aware that every man of my age thinks he is one. It is this opinion which gives to old men that air of condescension, that tone of gentle patronage, as if to say, "See how much I know about life and its duties!" But I have noticed on youthful faces at such times a painful look of inquiry, as if they would ask, "Well, if you know so much why have you so little to show for it?" Ah! that is the question. How many centuries is it since Plato was writing those immortal dialogues which have bewitched the minds of men from his age to ours, but have left us still struggling to make knowledge and conduct go hand in hand, and wisdom and character true reflections of each other. Nothing is so easy as to state sound ethical doctrines, and nothing so hard as to live up to them. I suppose that more than one-half the literature of the world consists of good advice; the rest is the story of its success or failure. Innumerable hands have traced the roads that lead to happiness and peace, but how few there be who have not missed the way.

I shall summon you to-night to a course of living which is filled with inspiring promises; but when I think of the mistakes you will probably make, and of those I have certainly made, my lips almost refuse to speak and I can only stammer as did George Eliot's Theophrastus Such, when he said to his hearers, " Dear blunderers, I am one of you." Some of you will, perhaps, never be wiser than you are now. I wish I could be sure you would never be less wise. It is one of the truths I implicitly believe, that the saddest mistake men make is not by failing to learn, but by foolishly thinking they must *unlearn*; by giving up the truer charts and guides, the clearer stars by which they sailed in youth.

It is not for me to enter the domain of religion nor to trench upon that ground which is occupied by better men who have been specially called to the work. I speak only of the life that now is. And this is the lesson I give you: Dwell in the kingdom of light. And where is that kingdom? Where are its boundaries? What cities are builded within it? What hills and plains and mountain slopes gladden the eyes of its possessors? Be patient my young enthusiast. Do not hasten to search for it. It is here. The kingdom of light, like the kingdom of Heaven, is within you.

And what do I mean by the kingdom of light? I mean that realm of which a quaint old poet sang those quaint old lines:

"My mind to me a kingdom is,
Such perfect joy therein I find."

I mean that invisible commonwealth which outlives the storms of ages; that empire more ancient than the east; that state whose armaments are thoughts; whose weapons are ideas; whose trophies are the pages of the world's great masters. The kingdom of light is the kingdom of the intellect, of the imagination, of the heart, of the spirit and the things of the spirit. And why, perhaps you will ask, do you make this appeal to us, who as students, as members of the fraternity of letters, are already dedicated to high purposes, and enrolled among those who stand for the nobler and better side of human life? Take it not amiss if I tell you frankly, I do not feel sure that you are; and besides, if you will pardon my plainness of speech, I must remind you that not all who stand in the ranks to-day will be found there a dozen years hence; not all who start with the column follow the colors through the afternoon of the march.

Why do you become students? Why are you members of these societies that cultivate art and eloquence and keep your hearts fresh with the dew of the humanities? Some there are, I fear, who look upon education simply as a weapon that will give them an advantage in what we call the battle of life. If this be your motive, you are not in the Kingdom. For, while knowledge is a tremendous force, and gives its possessor a great advantage over his unskilled adversary, yet it is more than this; it *must* be more, or it is hardly worth having. Its true value is that it is a stimulus to your own betterment, an incentive; and, believe me, it is also a reward. We must learn to pitch our lives to that grand key-note in one of Matthew Arnold's sonnets:

"The aids to noble life are all within."

There is another reason why I make this appeal to you. In the intellectual as well as the theological world, there is a tendency to backsliding; that fatal weakness which turns the feet backward and downward to the lowlands of gloom and despair. The young are almost always heroic. But the blood grows thin with age, and the resolute heart timid and fearful. At twenty you gaze upon the planets in the upper sky; but at forty, perhaps, you will be groping wearily along by some pallid light your own weak hands have kindled. The tempter marches side by side with the every human soul. And this ordeal which comes to all will come to you. In your ear there will be whisperings of a career; of a life not troubled by youthful traditions; of an existence which takes no thought to separate the things that are God's from the things that are Mammon's. Whoever the tempter may be, he is your enemy. He is your enemy because he has told you what is not true, and what, thank Heaven! never can be true. Human life, if it is to be better than that of the brutes, must be consecrated to something higher than itself.

I have appealed to you for what I have called the intellectual life. By the intellectual life I mean that course of living which recognizes always and without ceasing, the infinite value of the mind; which gives to its cultivation a constant and enthusiastic devotion; which in good and evil days clings to it with growing and abiding love. I beg of you not to suppose that it is based upon a college diploma, or that it is confined to what is known as the learned professions—law, medicine and theology; for it is sadly true that many who are enrolled in their ranks have not the slightest kinship with an intellectual life.

The Kingdom of Light is open to all who *seek* the light. This may seem a mere truism, since everyone admits the superiority of the mental over the physical nature. But that is where the danger lies. All admit it, and how very few act upon it. How many men and women do you know, who, after they have, as the phrase goes, finished their education, ever give it another serious thought? They have no time; no time to live, but only to exist. Do not misunderstand me: I do not expect, nor do I think it possible, that the great majority of people can make intellectual improvement their first and only aim. God's wisdom has made the law that we must dig and delve, must work with the hands and bend the back to the burden that is laid upon it. We must have bread; but how inexpressibly foolish it is to suppose that we can live by bread alone. Granting all that can be claimed for lack of time; for the food and clothing to be bought, and the debts to be paid, the truth remains—

and I beg you to remember it—the person who allows his mental and spiritual nature to stagnate and decay, does so, not for want of time, but for want of inclination. The farm, the shop and the office are not such hard masters as we imagine. We yield too easily to their sway, and set them up as rulers when they ought to be servants. There is no vocation, absolutely none, that cuts off entirely the opportunities for intellectual development. For my part I would rather have been Charles Lamb than the Duke of Wellington, and his influence in the world is incalculably the greater of the two. And yet he was but a clerk in the India House, poor in pocket, but rich beyond measure in his very poverty, whose jewels are not in the goldsmith's list. The problem of life is to rightly adjust the prose to the poetry; the sordid to the spiritual; the common and selfish to the high and benificent, forgetting not that these last are incomparably the more precious.

Modern life is a startling contradiction. Never were colleges so numerous, so prosperous, so richly endowed as now. Never were public schools so well conducted, or so largely patronized. But yet, what Carlyle calls "the mechanical spirit of the age" is upon us. The commercial spirit too, is with us, holding its head so high that timid souls are frightened at its pretensions. It is the scholar's duty to set his face resolutely against both.

I can never be the apostle of despair. The colors in the morning and the evening sky are brilliant yet. But I fear the scholar is not the force he once was, and will again be when the nineteenth century, or the next one, gets through its carnival of invention and construction. We have culture; what we need is the love of culture. We have knowledge; but our prayer should be: Give us the love of knowledge. I may be wrong, but I sometimes wish Nature would be more stingy of her secrets. She has given them out with so lavish a hand that some men think the greatest thing in the world is to persuade her to work in some newly invented harness. Edison and the other wizards of science have almost succeeded in making life automatic. Its chord is set to a minor key. Plain living and high thinking, that once went together, are transformed into high living and very plain thinking. The old-time simplicity of manners, the modest tastes of our fathers, have given way to the clang and clash, the noise and turbulence that characterize the age. We know too much; and too little. We know evolution; but who can tell us when, or how, or why, it came to be the law? We accept it as a great scientific truth, and as such it should be welcomed. But life has lost something of its zest, some of the glory that used to be in it, since we were told—though I do not believe it—that mind is only an emanation of matter, a force or principle mechanically produced by molecular motion within the brain. When the telephone burst upon us a few years ago, the world was delighted and amazed. And yet we were not needing telephones half as much so we were needing men; men, who, by living above the common level, should exalt and dignify human life. I sometimes think it wise to close the patent office in Washington, and to say to the tired brains of the inventors, "Rest and be refreshed." We hurry on to new devices which shall be ears to the deaf, and eyes to the blind, and feet to the halt; but meantime the poems are unwritten, and hearts that are longing for one strain of the music they used to hear are told to be satisfied with the great achievements of the nineteenth century. The wisest of the Greeks taught that the ideal is the only true real; and Emerson, our American seer, who sent forth from Concord his inspiring oracles, taught the same. I may be wrong, but I cannot help thinking that neither hereafter, nor here, does salvation lie in wheat, or corn, or iron.

Again I must plead that you will take my words as I mean them. I do not mean to preach a gospel of mere sentiment, nor of an inane impracticable dilettanteism. The Lord put it in my way to learn, long ago, that we cannot eat poetry, or art and sunbeams. And yet I hold it true, now and always, that life without these things is shorn of more than half its value. The ox and his master differ little in dignity, if neither rises above the level of the stomach and the manger.

The highest use of the mind is not mere logic, the almost mechanical function of drawing conclusions from facts. Even lawyers do that; and so also, to some extent as naturalists tell us, do the horse and the dog. The human intellect is best used when its possessor suffers it to reach out beyond its own environment into the realm where God has placed truth and beauty and the influences that make for righteousness. There is no such thing as a common or humdrum life unless we make it so ourselves. The rainbow and the rose give their colors to all alike. The sense of beauty that is born in every soul pleads for permission to remain there. Cast it out, and not all the skill of Edison can replace it.

It is the imagination, or perhaps I should say the imaginative faculty, that most largely separates man from the lower animals, and which also divides the higher from the lower order of men. We all respect the multiplication table, and find in it about the only platform upon which we can agree to stand; but he would be a curiously incomplete man to whose soul it could bring the rapture that comes from reading "Hamlet" or "In Memoriam." The thoughts that console and elevate are not those the world calls practical. Even in the higher walks of science, where the mind enlarges to the scope of Newton's and Kepler's great discoveries, the demonstrated truth is not the whole truth, nor the best truth. As Prof. Everett, of Harvard, has finely said in a recent work, "science only gives us hints of what, by a higher method, we come to know. The astronomer tells us he has swept the heavens with his telescope and found no God." But "the eye of the soul" outsweeps the telescope, and finds, not only in the heavens but everywhere, the presence that is eternal. The reverent soul seeking for the power that makes for righteousness, will not find it set down in scientific formula. I hold it to be the true office of education to stimulate the higher intellectual faculties; to give the mind something of that perfection which is found in finely tuned instruments that need only to be touched to give back noble and responsive melody. There is a music that has never been named; and yet so deep a meaning has it that the very stars keep time to its celestial rhythm.

> "There's not the smallest orb which thou beholds't,
> But in his motion like an angel sings,
> Still quiring to the young-eyed cherubim;
> Such harmony is in immortal souls."

I do not claim that scholarship, as it is commonly understood, scholarship merely as such, can, or does, open the gates of the invisible world, or open your hearts to the beauty that is everywhere. But I do claim that in so far as it falls short of this, in so far as it hinders or obstructs, or diverts you from it, it has failed of its purpose. This college which you rightly love and cherish; this college and the other institutions of learning throughout the country, do a good work when they teach you facts, and how to apply them; but they do a greater and better work when they fill the hearts of their students with a consuming love for the things that cannot be computed, nor reckoned nor measured. In the daily papers you may read the last quotations of stocks and bonds; but once upon a time a little band of listeners heard the words, "Are not two sparrows sold for a farthing?" and went away with a lesson whose meaning Wall street has yet to learn.

And now you are asking, "Do you expect us to earn money by following these shadowy and intangible sentiments, which, however noble, are not yet current at the store and market? We must eat though poetry and art and music perish from the earth." Yes, so it would seem, but only *seem*. I cannot tell you *why*, but I am sure that he who remembers that something divine in him is mixed with the clay, shall find the way opened for both the divine and the earthly. You will not starve for following the Light. But I beg of you to remember that this is not a question of incomes or profits. The things I plead for are not set down in ledgers. How hard to think of the unselfish and the ultimate, instead of the personal and immediate! Even unto Jesus they came and inquired, "Who is first in the Kingdom of Heaven?" It is not strange then that we do not willingly give up personal advantages here. But in the Kingdom of Light, in the life I am asking you to lead, nothing can be taken from you that can be compared with what you will receive. It is quite likely you may be poor, though I am afraid you will not be, for in the nineteenth century, no man is safe from sudden wealth; but a worse calamity could befall you than poverty. St. Francis of Assisi, as Renan has said, was, next to Jesus, the sweetest soul that ever walked this earth, and he condemned himself to hunger and rags. I do not advise you to follow him through the lonely forest, and into the shaded glen where the birds used to welcome him to be their friend and companion; but I do most assuredly think it better to live as he did, on bread and water and the cresses that grew by the mountain spring, than to give up the glory and the joy of the higher life. In the Kingdom of Light there are friendships of inestimable value; friendships that are rest unto the body and solace to the soul that is troubled. When Socrates was condemned, how promptly and how proudly his spirit rose to meet the decree of the judges, as he told them of the felicity he should find in the change that would give him the opportunity of listening to the enchanting converse of Orpheus and Musæus and Hesiod and Homer. Such companionship is ours through the instrumentality of books. Here, even in this western land, the worthies of every age will come to your firesides; will travel with you on the distant journey; will abide with you wherever your lot may be cast. And the smaller the orbit in which you move, the more contracted the scale of your personal relation, the more valuable and the more needful are those sweet relationships which James Martineau so aptly calls "the friendships of history." In a strain of unrivaled elevation of thought and purity of language, he says: "He that cannot leave his workshop or his village, let him have his passport to other centuries, and find communion in a distant age; it will

enable him to look up into those silent faces that cannot deceive, and
take the hand of solemn guidance that will never mislead or betray.
The ground-plot of a man's own destiny may be closely shut in, and the
cottage of his rest small; but if the story of this Old World be not quite
strange to him—if he can find his way through its vanished cities to hear
the pleadings of justice or watch the worship of the gods; if he can visit
the battlefields where the infant life of nations has been baptized in
blood; if he can steal into the prisons where the lonely martyrs have
waited for their death; if he can walk in the garden or beneath the porch
where the lovers of wisdom discourse, or be a guest at the banquet where
the wine of their high converse passes around; if the experience of his
own country and the struggles that consecrate the very soil beneath his
feet are no secret to him, and he can listen to Latimer at Paul's Cross,
and tend the wounded Hampden in the woods of Chalgrove, and gaze,
as upon familiar faces, at the portraits of More and Bacon, of Vane and
Cromwell, of Owen, Fox and Baxter—he consciously belongs to a grander
life than could be given by territorial possession; he venerates an ances-
try auguster than a race of kings; and is richer in the sources of character than many a merchant prince or railway monarch.   Hence the advantage which *human studies* possess over every other form of science;
the sympathy with man over the knowledge of nature."

Some there are, no doubt, who believe that intellectual culture does
not make men better or happier, and that the conscience and moral faculties are set apart from merely mental attributes.   But surely you have
not accepted such a false and narrow view.   Unless colleges are a foolish and expensive luxury; unless civilization is worthless; unless the centuries that have witnessed the upward stride of humanity have been
wasted; unless the savage, chattering incantations to his fetich, is a nobler
product of the race than a Milton, a Wilberforce, an Emerson or a Low-
ell, then heart and mind, morality and education *do* go together in true
and loyal companionship.   The trouble of to-day, as I have tried to show,
is not that we have too much culture, but too much bending of the knee
to purely material results; too much worship of the big and not enough
of the great.   I live in hope that the students of Knox College will help
to correct this evil.   I must, however, confess that when I see young
men and women going out from their college life into that other and far
different one that awaits them, I always feel a little twinge of pain, a
premonition of danger, a fear that in spite of all their high resolves, the
demon of the nineteenth century will lead them captive.   And that is

what I meant when I spoke of backsliding. The Kingdom of Light is not as populous as it would be if all who once set their faces thither-ward had pressed forward without turning.

It will be the fate of most of you to work with hand and brain; but do not forget that even in this short life a successfully conducted bank, or a bridge that you have built, or a lawsuit you have won, have in themselves little of special significance or value. Very common men have done all these things. When I hear the glorification of the last twenty years, of the fields subdued, the roads built, the fortunes accumulated, the factories started, I say to myself, all these are good, but not good enough that we should make ourselves hoarse with huz-zas, or that we should suppose for a moment they belong to the high-er order of achievements. Sometimes, too, when I hear the noisy clamor over some great difficulty that has been conquered, I think of James Wolfe under the walls of Quebec, repeating sadly those solemn lines of Gray's Elegy:

"The boast of heraldry, the pomp of pow'r,
And all that beauty, all that wealth e'er gave,
Await alike th' inevitable hour,
The paths of glory lead but to the grave."

And I think also how he turned to his officers with that pathetic prevision of the death that was to come to-morrow on the Heights of Abraham, and said, "I would rather have written that poem than to take Quebec." And he was right.

Indeed, if we but knew it, the citadel that crowns the mountain's brow, nay, the mountains themselves, ancient, rugged, motionless, are but toys compared with the silent, invisible, but eternal structure of God's greatest handiwork, the mind.

I pray you remember there is, if you will search for it, something ennobling in every vocation; in every enterprise which engages the ef-forts of man. Do you think Michael Angelo reared the dome and painted those immortal frescoes simply because he had a contract to do so? Was the old soldier who died at Marathon or Gettysburg thinking of the wages the state had promised him? Be assured, young ladies and gentlemen, that whatever fate is to befall you, nothing so bad can come as to sink into that wretched existence where everything is for-gotten but the profit of the hour: the food, the raiment, the handful of silver, the ribbon to wear on the coat. It is but an old story I am telling you; but I console myself with the reflection that it cannot be told too often, and only by telling is it kept fresh in the memory and in the heart. I wish I knew the secret of words. Then would I make you see the surpassing value of the life I have tried to portray. I wish I knew the secret of art. Then would I paint a picture that should be the image of joy and beauty, and behind the canvas, not seen, but known by the subtle intuitions of the mind, there should throb the living heart of an ideal life. Then would I ask you to be true to that ideal, knowing that it can never be false to you. The world will go on buying and selling, hoping and fearing, loving and hating, and you will be in the throng; but in God's name turn not away from the light, nor from the kingdom that is in the midst of the light.

You are young, you have faith; but I dare not ask you how much. For faith, however strong it may be, has its tides; and many a gallant bark has gone down in sight of the coast that seemed to beckon with · its welcoming smiles. I consider that life wrecked, though it can count its millions and has built cities and removed mountains, if it has lost sight of the upper lights. You think no such fate can come to you; but so has thought every high-souled youth from the age of Pericles to the present.

In every street shadows are walking who were once like you, young, hopeful and confident. Nay! they are not shadows; but ghosts, dead, years ago, in everything but the mere physical portion of existence. They go through the regular operations of trade and traffic, the office and the court; but they are not living men.   They are but bones and skeletons rattling along in a melancholy routine, which has in it neither life nor the spirit of life. It is a sad picture, but saddest because it is true. They knew what happy days were, when like you, they walked in pleasant paths and felt in their hearts the freshness of the spring. But contact with the world was too much for them. Hesitation and doubt drove out loyalty and faith. They listened to the voice of worldly wisdom as Othello listened to Iago, and the end of the story is:

"Put out the light, and then,—put out the light."

I appeal to the students of Knox College to be worthy of its great founder. You have, by your enrollment here, been called and numbered with the elect.   You are hostages to art and letters; to high aims and noble destinies. You may be false, but if some are not faithful, truth and liberty and the best of civilization will be lost, or in danger of being lost. In every ship that sails there must be some to stay by the craft; some to speak the word of cheer; some to soothe the fears of the timorous and affrighted. When Paul was journeying to Italy on that memorable voyage which changed the destinies of the world, the mariners were frightened as the storm came on, and were casting the boats over to seek safety they knew not whither; but Paul said to the centurion and to the soldiers, "Except these abide in the ship ye cannot be saved."

I call upon the students of Knox College to stay by the ship. It is because I believe so strongly in the saving power of the intellectual life upon the institutions of society, and upon the welfare of individuals, that I have urged you so earnestly to be loyal to it. The fortunes of science, art, literature and government are indissolubly linked with it. The center and shrine of the most potent influences are not the seats of commerce and capital. The village of Concord, where Emerson, Hawthorne, Alcott and Thoreau lived, was in their day, and will long continue to be, a greater force in this nation than New York and Chicago added to each other. You must rest in the assured faith that whoever may *seem* to rule, the thinker is, and always will be, the master. He can well afford to let the man of affairs enjoy his dream of dominion, for the law of the universe is that all things must serve the silent but imperious power of thought.

Those of you who have read Auerbach's great novel remember the motto from Goethe on the title page:

"On every height there lies repose."

Rest! how eagerly we seek it! How sweet it is when we are tired of the fret and worry of life. But remember, I pray you, that it dwells above the level in the serene element that reaches to the infinities. Only there is heard the music of the choir invisible; only there can you truly know the rest, the peace and joy of those who dwell in the Kingdom of Light.